Remember

Remember

by

Barbara Southard

Allbook Books

Selden, NY, USA

Copyright © 2008 by Barbara Southard.
Cover photograph by Barbara Southard.
All rights reserved.

Except for the quoting of brief passages, these poems may not be reproduced in any manner for publication, electronic or otherwise, without the written permission of the publisher.

First edition.

Marvin Bell, excerpt from "Eastern Long Island" from *Nightworks: Poems 1962-2000*. Copyright © 2000 by Marvin Bell. Reprinted with the permission of Copper Canyon Press, www.coppercanyonpress.org.

Printed in the United States of America.

Published by: Allbook Books
    PO Box 562
    Selden, NY 11784
    www.allbook-books.com

ISBN-10: 0-9743603-9-2
ISBN-13: 978-0-9743603-9-3

CONTENTS

Neighborhood Men	13
I Look at the Loon	14
Building a Path from Collected Bricks	15
Rowing at 3 A.M.	16
Migrating Monarchs Mixing with Gulls	17
Benches at Cedar Beach	18
Circle	20
Nunley's Carousel	21
Shoreline	22
Birds in the Parking Lot	23
Ice	24
On the Bay	25
Living—Watching	29
Beach Parking Lot	30
Labor Pool Workers	31
The Same Dreams	32
Large Dreams	33
I Was Here. This Is Me.	34
Late-night Phone Calls	35
"Light as a cork I danced upon the waves"	36
Marks	37
One Night in St. Augustine	38
Confectioners	39
Sumps	40
Remember	41

Moment	45
Knowing	46
Devotional	47
New Paths	48
Old Woman in the Sun	49
Old Woman and Old Man	50
There's No Knowing How the Day Will Begin or End	52
What Makes One Person Love Another?	53
Kenai Peninsula at 11 P.M.	54
Passage	55
The Back of Barry's Head	56
Where Poetry Begins	57
Corpus Callosum	61
Blue Egg	62
At Nightfall at the Outskirts of the City Two Children Are Threatened by a Nightingale	63
"My Pretties"	64
Francis Bacon at Work	65
Dan's Portrait	66
Poem Notes and Acknowledgments	68
About the Author	71
Allbook Books information	72

For Michael

It takes longer to come to joy now
but then the golden light races
across the desert floor
faster than a coyote can run
and the morning sun
scrambles over the mountain
drenching me in its brilliance.
This is what you lived for.

*. . .here are torn memories of inlets and canals,
of ponds, bays, creeks, coves, spits and sandbars . . .*

— Marvin Bell
from "Eastern Long Island" in *Nightworks*

Neighborhood Men
Miller Place

What are they building now
—and how many projects can they find
on such a short narrow path of a road?
The buzz of saw, sound of hammers
is heard through the days
and the blue-jeaned, flannel-shirted men
spend their hours working together:
the sound of a slap on the back,
full-belly laugh, pop of tab-top cans—
clang of metal against metal
when tossed in empty.
They walk by the house carrying tools
to fix a floor, stop a leak, cut tree trunks
into pieces for burning. There's a sense
of safety here: wood, hammer, saw.

I Look at the Loon

and want to feel
the exquisite patterning
of white rectangles
on glossy blacks
against my skin.

I want to become
the white speckles drifting
through black blackness
pressing against a downy white chest
against my skin.

I want to merge
with the perfectly aligned bars
of white whiteness
circling a neck of black blackness
against my skin.

I want feathers
to sprout from my pores
like wildflowers
after a rain—
my eyes
turn to rubies.

    [Poet's Note]
    Common loons come down from the Adirondacks every winter.
    Many of them can be seen on Long Island Sound.

Building a Path from Collected Bricks
Miller Place

I take out my tools, line them up
then choose which brick fits with another:
dusty rose next to madder lake, pebbly
nuance next to smooth—
slight slope, sand, arc of curve.

The pyramid of bricks dwindles
to an assortment of earlier rejects
now seen with different eyes,
irregularities suddenly desirable:
triangular shapes nudged
into accommodating crevices;
the worn oblong brick, surfaced
with a white snowstorm of pebbles
placed next to shades of burnt umber.

Tides continue to scrub the shoreline,
dig up bricks once burrowed
next to old ship parts, bones, coins,
anchors, tree trunks, turtle skulls—
a gold ring tossed far into the surf.

Rowing at 3 A.M.
Freeport

When oars slip into the water
waking drifting jellyfish
stars slide down from the morning sky
mingle with blue claws searching
for their morning meal
while mussels hiss from muddy banks
and the lopsided moon shoots ribbons
of silver across the canal—

dark houses on each side
like ancient amphibians
waiting for the morning sun
to touch their backs, start the day.

A boat, coming in from a night's fishing
searchlights the docks for mooring
sending killies for cover
until it's dark, still, once again—
amoebic-scented seawater
impregnating the air.

Migrating Monarchs Mixing with Gulls
Mount Sinai Harbor

So haphazard, our transformations
—bacchanalian feast laid out
on a conveyor belt, velocity increasing
sensory input too swift for ease:
air filled with wings and things—
Bang! shells dropped from such a height
bubble of blue sky, flurry of orange
sashaying past birds swooping down,
mantling the goldenrod, bleached beach grass—
all inside this spell-bound water dome.

Benches at Cedar Beach

        Winter

It started with one bench facing the sound.
A plaque was added   *in memory of. . .*
then another bench.

They are spreading like milkweed seeds
toward the fishing pier
in memory of. . . in memory of. . .

A decorated cedar tree stands in front of them
as if angels could sit and watch
the silver garlands catching the sun's light.

        Spring

March sun has burned through to April.
The cedar trees have new seed cones,
turning their bronzed foliage to green.

Rabbits are playing Red Light/Green Light
along the path
blending with beach and brush.

Silver garlands have been replaced
with pastel ribbons. They flutter in the breeze.
A fresh yellow rose shouts from a bench.

Summer

Mourning doves sit in the trees singing the blues
with the foghorn blowing in the harbor.
Seabirds add a dissonant note to the melody.

Azure berries glow like miniature moons
against the dense foliage of the cedar trees,
their own universe complete.

A child runs ahead of her mother,
chooses a bench to sit on, her face
as luminescent as a pearl plucked from a shell.

Autumn

Poison ivy lights up the dunes with fluorescent reds.
A few pale pink beach roses linger on
and beach plum plants hang low with fruit.

Feeding birds are wild with ecstasy, littering
the path with pits stripped clean.
The oblique sun drenches the trees in gold.

Beach glass, carefully bound, hangs from the cedar tree.
Ribbons fade, like plants reaching dormancy.
The benches wait.

Circle
Sound Beach

From far off, the gull looks like a mound
of feathers on the bitter-cold beach,
eyes so alive atop a pile of useless fluff,
alone at the edge of the sea,
tide rising, pushing him back and forth,
clouds racing by.

To be so utterly alone, yet so alive.

He looks up to watch his flock pass by,
sees one turn back, fly round in circles
calling out again and again.

She flies one last circle above his head,
wings beating against his ruin—
then away from his watching eyes,
gray feathers animated by white,
mirror to clouds above
darkness of pebbles on the shore.

Nunley's Carousel
Baldwin, New York — 1940-1995

Oh, to feel the joy of it once again—
wild wobbly horse, melody of organ,
xylophone, sensual drum—body trembling
with every lift up, out, to life itself.

I searched for the outside horse:
the large one, with head tossed back
white teeth gleaming; sat high
in the saddle, holding on tight,
waiting for the sound of a bell

the first shaky wobble—lurch forward
then faster, eyes turned to kaleidoscopes,
music gathering momentum, drums
keeping beat—up—up, wings sprouting
from the center of my back—

a divine reach for the brass ring
with each rotation around the sun.

Oh, joy—cold shock of metal
clutched in a sweaty palm—
promise of one more ride
on the outside horse—the large one,
with head tossed back, white teeth gleaming.

Shoreline

The shoreline has become less monotonous—
last year, straight as a plumb line
with a slight curve toward the horizon

now, gouged out—leaving French curves,
low dunes covered with boat parts,
unmoored anchors, buoys.

It's as if whispers have become
insistent loud conversations,
occasional tantrums.

The full moon brings oracular tides
yet higher, leaving dug-out channels
of rushing seawater—
flooded roads near marshes.

Birds in the Parking Lot
Amityville

Each morning, when I pull in to work at eight,
I hear birds singing in the parking lot.
While they are out there gathering together
like the tribes of Abraham, feeling the air turn
from August heat to autumn chill, I am
in the grips of microbe-filled ducts pushing frigid air
into my cubicle, flickering fluorescent lights, my sun.

While they are out there, flying and feasting
for the long flight south, I am anchored
to the cold glare of a square screen, sending
false messages to the world. While they
are out there, in the golden gleam of summer's sun,
I am pinned to paved roads and alleyways, inching
my way to work and back—to work and back.

Ice
Big Fresh Pond

If we hadn't been walking nearby
at precisely that time
we wouldn't have heard cascades
of musical notes, a series of chimes,
soft popping—melodies drifting
through swaying pines.

We wouldn't have seen
delicate membranes of ice
tremble and crack
around the verge of the pond
until water, ice and land
settled back into quiet symmetry.

On the Bay
Shinnecock Bay

Rain comes down hard through thick briny air,
large glistening arrows
reverting back to their source,
like salmon returning to their place of birth.

If you stay out here long enough,
you can pick up countless patterns
of replication, invisible connections
binding one to another.

Does the fish beneath my boat
feel pain?
What do I owe the horseshoe crab
for my existence?

We are all beneficiaries of our beginnings,
cousins to the terrapin
poking its head out of marsh water,
soul-mate to swans nurturing their young.

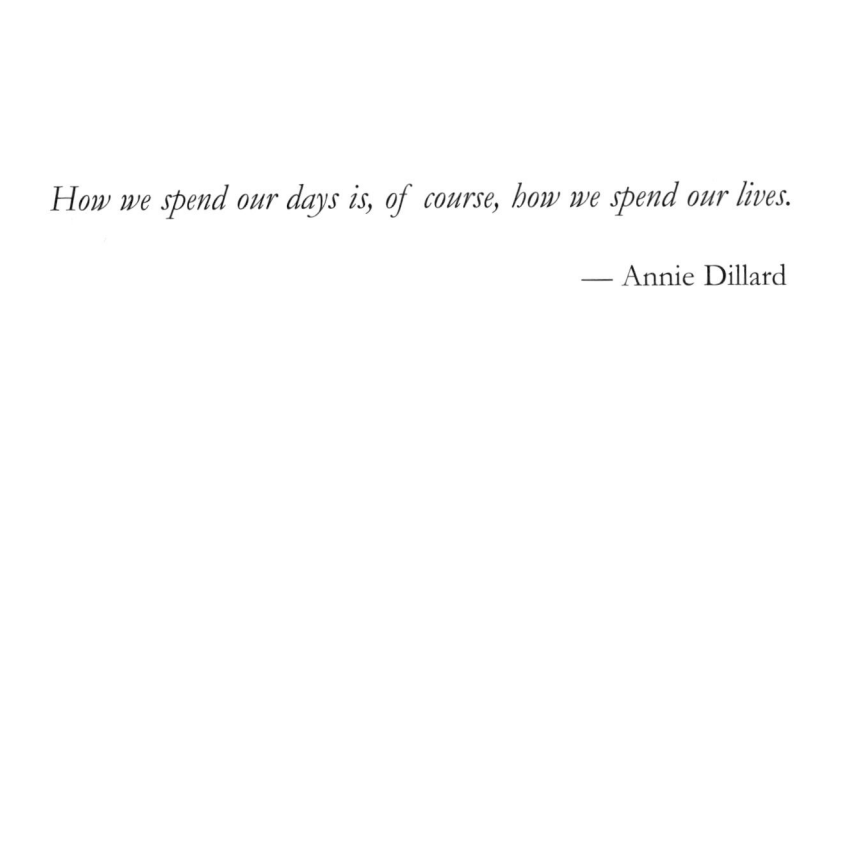

How we spend our days is, of course, how we spend our lives.

— Annie Dillard

Living—Watching

Words might capture a part of it.
A painting might freeze an hour's sunlight
slanting across a grove of trees—
but it is living, watching, that matters most:

to feel the warm sun sliding across your back,
watch a progression of clouds
move across a full moon,
see the color of bark on a tree change to plum
when the sun hides behind tumultuous branches:

to be an envoy between what is seen
—changing with each blink of an eye—
to freeze just one of those fractals in time
and give back bits and pieces of the whole
like tattered rags skittering across the ground.

Beach Parking Lot

Every day, cars line up
facing out toward the sea,
keeping company with the
seagulls braving the wind.
One man sips beer from a can;
another lets the radio beat a tune,
the soft thumps sounding like
huge bird wings beating the air.

They look out to sea, searching
for something lost somewhere
in that tidal expanse:
for a glimpse of their past
before memory or words—
seeking a way back—
as their eyes follow the sailboat
inching its way across the horizon.

Labor Pool Workers
Jacksonville, Florida

They start arriving before light, climb
into vans, fan out through the city
to dig holes, scrape paint off ships, clean out
toxic tanks in the mills—lesions roiling up
on scarred skin, battered hands—
caustic chemicals, blistering heat
—indecipherable faces darkened by sun.

From four in the afternoon until eight,
they roll in, spill out of vans, pick up
their day's pay
—bandaged hand, bent back, favored foot—
They spider out along 8th Street, make their way
home, catch some sleep, then back before light
—each day, new faces mixed with old—
mixture of sweat, muscle and bone.

The Same Dreams
Jacksonville, Florida

Downtown, sun bleaches skeleton houses
and front porches hold the weight of refugees
from other lives—all, who had somewhere, at some time,
a father, mother, sister, brother, son, daughter
or childhood friend—all gathered together near 8th Street
where the labor pool sends out tentacles
extracting every last morsel, leaving mounds
of emptied shells to be swept up, sorted out like field beans
—where men, who hope for no more than a day's work
are happy when a dollar falls into their hands
and any business that needs a dirty job done can count its money
because the hospital on 8th Street
takes in the uninsured—where the sound of helicopters
landing on the roof, sirens wailing, waiting rooms
filled to capacity, is the closest thing
to a third world country until Katrina hit New Orleans.

Downtown, where people from uptown are buying up
bare-boned houses, windows spilling tears over years
of sudden deaths, lost friendships, quiet departures,

days running into weeks, into years—the same dreams
running through lives—the same dreams
as if memory is erased before next day's sunrise.

Large Dreams
traveling around U.S.A.

I passed by a three-story igloo
off Highway 3 in Alaska
somewhere north of Anchorage
where someone dreamed large,
but birds now fly
in and out of broken windows—

passed by ghost towns
in the middle of woods,
at the end of dusty roads
in deserts, left to winds
rubbing against walls,
wearing them down
until they collapse into heaps,
leaving a fireplace or chimney
standing like sentries
guarding past lives
now mingled together

and rains wash away debris
from abandoned mine shafts,
closed strip malls,
resorts in the mountains—
where no one visits
but deer, moles, occasional hikers—
and trees will push their roots
through walkways, bottoms
of faded swimming pools,
abandoned parking lots, leaving
objects to be picked up by curious
children, dreaming large dreams.

I Was Here. This Is Me.

A pile of rocks by the river, driftwood
constructions on a wind-swept beach

names on the wall of a bathroom stall
or carved in the trunk of an old oak tree

striated markings on subway windows
spray-painted tags on sides of bridges

block letters in shadows, throw-ups
and stickers: *I was here. This is me.*

Proclamations of love on overpass banners
initials incised in cement foundations

or interiors of caves, carvings
on tables or tops of mountains

abandoned houses, time-lined tunnels
or prison walls; signals sent

through the web, bottles dropped in the sea:
   I was here. This is me.

Late-night Phone Calls

Could it be a barometric shift in the atmosphere,
a wobble on Earth's axis, or a hesitation
in the planets' movement around the sun?
Could it be mere coincidence, or that potent mixture
coursing through veins shaping our perceptions?

The phone brings questions that cannot be answered,
daily reminders of limitations, interminable decline
—impermanence—bloom of childhood buried
under layers of living, floating in and out of memory.

All we can offer is our presence, an ear as witness.
The air will lose its trembling, simmer down,
turn placid as a just-fed baby—each day, calm once again
until the next constellation drifts in,
bringing questions that cannot be answered.

"Light as a cork I danced upon the waves"

He used his body as paintbrush and pen
taking chances—as all artists must—mistakes
not as easily crossed out or painted over
—yet his turbulence could stir up the dead
give them another shot at rapture.
They would have taken him for a crazed terrorist
if he had lived long enough—
checked his shoes for bombs when he boarded
the plane on the west coast
with a string of garlic around his neck,
a wolf's tooth from the Siskiyou mountains
in his pocket and a backpack filled with Dungeness crabs.

Some people aren't meant to grow old—doesn't suit them.
They burn bright, leave a trail seen for miles, change orbit
when life gets dull—then they're gone—leaving us behind.

Marks

There's something to be said
for marks made by use—

the darkened handle on a hammer,
a wedding band reduced to a sliver
of gold, concaved cutting board
hanging on the kitchen wall.

The finish is worn to bare wood
next to the old door knob
where knuckles have rubbed
for sixty years:

scrubby boy hands turning the latch
just for the joy of making things happen,
misshapen joints of an old man,
the first fumbling efforts of a small child.

One Night in St. Augustine

There was an old shack sitting on a dock.
There was the faint sound of music
leading us through the dark palmettos
towards a haze of light—
white gleam shifting into colors of the galaxies.
There was a clearing near the dock
filled with parked cars, vintage trucks
creating their own configuration,
like pick-up sticks dropped to the ground.

Inside the shack, rows of tables, a clear space
for the band twanging out tunes
—whirling tangle of arms, legs:
wild-haired children, weather-worn men,
skinny gray-haired folks, big-bellied women
all moving to the beat—
floorboards rebounding to stomping feet

and we wanted to stay in this place,
grow old together
dance to fiddles on Saturday nights
with the smell of marsh and fried fish
where wind rustles through spiky leaves.

Confectioners

I followed the scent of chocolate
to the open door of the confectioner's
breathed in
a window cracked open
fragrance of oak and pine seeping in
breathed in
wild beach roses
skin brushing against skin
breathed in
a fox running through woods
leaving no trace
breathed in
cornish hens roasting
the thinnest slice of apple pie
breathed in
the rawness of a rough ocean
sting of sand.

Sumps

Someone I know found God in a sump.
Another found a dead monkey
lying entangled with a dead raccoon.
One saw men hiding behind some trees,
another, turtles sunning on a log.

You'd be surprised what you find
once you climb that fence.
Just because sumps have fences
to keep people out, doesn't mean
nothing goes on in there.

If I were a cat or a fox, I'd wait until dark,
creep in, see what goes on. And when
I'm very old, I think I'll slip in through
a hole in the fence, instead of sitting
on the porch, watching the cars go by
on the road leading out of town.

Remember

Remember this
Junior Brown playing the blues.
Those leaves at dusk traveling
to the center of your soul
through conduits of deep crimson.

Store this
In some retrievable place,
like the glass dish placed
on the window sill, still holding
sea-washed stones from that little town
in Italy, where we walked through
the woods to swim in the sea.

Remember this
The hummingbird that pierced
your heart with beauty outside
the window of the café near the
Bay of Fundy—or the snow geese
rising up of one mind like Buddha
out of the marshes in coastal Virginia.

Store these
In some retrievable place,
to be brought back when your eyes
dim and your body no longer answers
your bidding—when ghosts of past
failures crowd out the incandescent
feel of a baby's hand in yours.

Remember these
The multitude of sacred moments
that marched onward from that first
sentient spark to the last flickering light.

Remember

*We all have our own patch to cultivate.
What's important is that we dig deep.*

— paraphrased from a speech by José Saramago

Moment

There is that moment
burrowed between clattering dishes
or a fence that needs mending
—when there is perfection,
like the flashing silver reflection
of a school of fish passing by

when clarity takes hold
and life throws a clue:
another peach to be plucked
all fragrant and soft, each bite sweet,
juice coursing down your face
like salty tears.

Knowing
for my daughters & daughters-in-law

An idea takes hold, grows larger
becomes an ideology
while a woman labors to give birth.
Is she thinking of good and evil,
rules of conduct, or has she traveled
further, where rhythmic forces
push   push   push life out
from its amniotic capsule
onto a planet where concepts soar
into uncharted fields—or plod worn paths.
She is occupied with a different part of her brain
where knowledge arrives in another form—
senses aligned to patterns of raindrops
falling back to the sea.
She lies there spent, infant in arms, knowing.

Devotional

Charleston in July has air so dense,
as if tiny marine organisms
are floating through, smelling
of crushed oyster shells, moss,
damp earth, decomposition.

Life cycle's evidence:
a vibrating closeness
to what can't be seen, yet is felt;
rapid return to the spirit,
pretense stripped of its safety,
layers peeled away
by the workings of heat, humidity.

Otters swim down the river, past
worn pathways, ancient brick walls
—muffled cries can be heard
from the marketplace.

New Paths

While awake, we guard our lives
    rationalize our thoughts
        keep busy

until someone asks a question
    and the answer
        gated in some dark recess

takes form, turns into words
    leaps uncensored
        into the light of day

or a thought sits pestering
    like a whining dog
        wanting a pat on the head

or in the dark quiet of early morning
    a dream bursts forth
        of such intensity

like the birth of stars, rearranging
    form and structure
        new paths forged in tangled woods.

Old Woman in the Sun

The old woman sat in the sun
remembering the time she knew
(just as violets know when it's time to grow)
she knew joy so imponderable
spreading through her body like
the sweetness of honeysuckle nectar
sipped as a child. She knew
she'd arrived in a place
time could never steal, nor change,
or death take away what she knew.

Everything after, a mere leap
from one lily pad to another—
a hollow log to rest in
between journeys into the unknown
where cosmic showers
explode from spiraling trajectories
in magnetic fields
where the flowering of an orange sun presses
against the horizon
where a pod of whales
sends messages—flukes raised in prayer.

Old Woman and Old Man

The old woman was burying her friend
from the old times. They were inseparable,
traveled the world together, rode rapids,
climbed volcanos to peer in—saw what
the earth looked like under the surface,
raised all that mischief in the Russian woods
frightening children until they ran away.
It was fun, something to do when nothing
was left but chew on some seal skin, dig
for potatoes, or meddle in family feuds.

The soil felt good in her hands
full of fat worms, busy organisms
balancing sky with ground.
An old man came over, sat down next to her
asked if he could share the space.
Start digging, she said. *I could use the help.*
Together, they dug a big hole
lowered her friend inside
although she had shrunk down
to almost nothing—
just a small bundle of black silk.

He arranged his war medals
in an intricate design on the black silk,
added a box of forbidden tears,
some post-traumatic stress dreams
tied with string.
She added boxes of teeth, bent bones
from shoes worn too small
bloodstained wedding sheets,
tears shed for dead children.

Together, they piled one object
on top of another,
their bones becoming lighter, like the bones
of flamingos, blue jays, house wrens.
They shed old feathers for new:
yellows and reds stolen from the sun,
umbers and greens gathered from the ground.

Together, they settled into an unfamiliar landscape.

There's No Knowing
How the Day Will Begin or End

Before dawn, the sharp ring of a phone
cuts through a carnal dream.

In the Andes, mummies emerge
from melted ice bearing news
and entombed insects
meld with plants from other ages
blurring beginnings and endings
like heavy rains blotting out words
on love letters. In the center of Antarctica
an ice core from a glacier whispers our future.
New evidence shows Ötzi the Iceman
was murdered with an arrow in the back.

Life comes to a lurching halt, just before
a family barbecue begins.

What Makes One Person Love Another?
for Ron, the father of our children

He knew his way around in the woods,
could start a fire from nothing, held
his first-born son in his arms while
running down a steep embankment
next to the rushing river where I stood,
terrified. A car engine appeared
beneath the bed, a motorcycle
in the bathtub. And why was I riding
behind a combine on a farm
somewhere on the west coast,
then hunting deer in the mountains
—yelling for them to run—
even though I had tired of potatoes.

Kenai Peninsula at 11 P.M.

The mountains
    reflect
        a golden glow from the sun
            low on the horizon

petal pink snow
    nested
        between plum colored rocks
            deep green of the tree line

the lake
    silver
        against a blue haze
            turning to dusky pink

turning to pale blue
    turning
        to buttery yellow
            low on the horizon.

The glacier nearby
    melts
        into the sea
            and the sea reaches out.

Passage

Touch me, the pity and comfort of skin.
— Janet Frame

It's good to take that black shapeless shadow
hold it to the light of day

where sharp edges emerge from dense overgrowth
in deep, concealed chambers

where images meander over fields of emotion
randomly plucking rays of light
from a sea of gray anemones waving for attention.

We are isolated in our own capsules of pain
turbulent hopes and desires

breaking through with the touch of a hand
or a sideways glance.

We are pebbles rolling along the bottom
of a fast moving stream
brushing against each other along the way.

The Back of Barry's Head

If you sit behind a boy an entire school year
even if you're only in 4th grade, the back
of his head provokes all kinds of interesting
observations, like the way the sun from the window
reflects off the shiny black slickness of his perfect
hair, or how the back of his neck, so luminous,
is covered with whirly designs of fine down,
or the way he moves his shoulder in a shrug
under his pressed pastel shirt and how his elbow
shakes back and forth, erasing mistakes.

I can't remember what I learned that year,
although I'm certain it was something useful,
nor can I remember any of the girls' names
I surely played with on the playground,
but I remember the back of Barry's head
in all its complexity, like last night's dream.

Where Poetry Begins
in the back seat of a car with a child, not yet two

She forms each word with care
   b i r d
lips pressed together
like tight buds ready to bloom.
From bird, she leaps to bumble bee,
then butterfly. Brows furrowed,
she pushes f f f f against bottom lip,
affixes it to iisshh—
   f i s h
she says, then says again and again:
sound   feel   form   flowing together.

We live in a fractured world.
I've always seen it as my role as an artist to attempt to make wholeness.

—Anish Kapoor

Corpus Callosum
after seeing an exhibit of Chuck Close's prints & paintings

Chuck Close said that his differently wired brain
led him to paint portraits in segments
because he had difficulty remembering faces.

I spent hours looking at his progressive proofs
in soft ground, his mezzotints, woodcuts, colors
layered upon colors in the most miraculous way.

It was as if I understood completely
the processes his brain went through.
It was as if I was running around in his head,

leaping from left hemisphere to right,
burrowing into his frontal lobes, exploding with joy.
I wondered if he ever got lost in parking garages,

how he kept on painting after his body failed him—
tying that brush to his hand in just the right way,
how he keeps going deeper and deeper,

bringing us along for the ride. I wondered
how he leapt over the great divide,
how he leapt over frozen limbs—
each grid a carefully constructed miracle.

Blue Egg

after seeing *At the Hub of Things,*
a sculpture by Anish Kapoor

This cut-in-half deep blue
egg-shaped object
is like a night sky devoid of stars
and if you look directly
into the center of its circle
you will feel shut out
as if there could not be entrance
to such density
yet if you move off-center
you will see a trace of edge
along the rim
and—gaining that knowledge—
you will look into its hub
with new eyes
and feel yourself entering
that deep blue interior
and from that deep blue interior
it will seem as if you are yet to be born
watching the world turn on its axis.

Then—step out—look back
and see a luminous object suspended,
there where you were
—so perfect in form
you unfold outside time and space.

At Nightfall at the Outskirts of the City
Two Children Are Threatened by a Nightingale
based on a painting by Max Ernst

Bulbs, blooming out of season.
Abandoned backhoes, half-dug foundations
rusted-out trailers, broken-down barns
corroded corrugated roofs.
Exiled families carrying snapped synaptic bridges.
Chemical streams coursing through veins
searching for a place to land.
A child harmed at a family gathering.
FOR SALE signs in yards strewn with tires
tractors, pickup trucks. A faded
Volkswagen bus sitting on jacks.
Stone projectiles from past centuries
burrowing in bones. Displaced elephants
exhibiting post-traumatic stress
—bees, abandoning their hives.

"My Pretties"
Emery Blagdon
1907-1986

If he takes iron laminates from transformers,
adds pop-tabs, strips of aluminum and bits
of foil—if he nails each component to scraps
of wood, adds small bottles, winds
each field of magic with unused wire,
hangs them from the ceiling and walls
of his shed in intricate patterns—if he adds
strings of Christmas lights to reflect off metal
and glass, paints the tops and bottoms
of his floorboards with geometric designs—
then he will disarm illness and death.
For who could not get well in such a room
filled with healing energy fields, created
from ineffable ardor? Who could resist
the allure of his rays of life, his lovely
constructions, his sculptures set on plinths?

Francis Bacon at Work

If you can talk about it, why paint it?
— Francis Bacon

Each day, on my way to work,
I'd pass an old house down the road
beyond a clearing, its swayed roof
scattered with branches from past storms
and even though my mind tells me
a house cannot be restless, this house
struggles to break loose
from its prison of glass, stone and wood.

A silvery wreath on the broken door
catches light from the transient sun
reflecting it back to the shaded yard
and, even though it wouldn't be possible,
I'd see him working inside, where
he stands in a shambles, brushing
the walls for color, searching—
for the eye, the mouth, the scream.

Dan's Portrait

Carted a horseshoe crab shell
From Shinnecock Bay,
Painted his essence
On its barnacled field—
Inscrutable
With swirls of stars
Spatters of paint
Finding places
Where they pleased—
Because space and thrust
Knows its own arc
Like perfect circles in sand
Drawn by sea grass
Blown by the wind.

Poem Notes and Acknowledgments

Page 36: "Light as a cork I danced upon the waves"
    The title of the poem is taken from a line in Rimbaud's "The Drunken Boat."

Page 64: Emery Blagdon spent thirty-three years of his life creating healing machines which he often referred to as "my pretties."

Grateful acknowledgment is made to the editors of the magazines and websites in which these poems first appeared: "Beach Parking" in *Long Island Quarterly*,
"Kenai Peninsula at 11 P.M." in *Long Island Quarterly* online,
"Circle" in *Performance Poets Association Literary Review - Volume 11*,
"Confectioners" and "Sumps" in *The Long-Islander*,
"The Back of Barry's Head" in *Long Island Sounds: 2005*,
"Large Dreams" in *Long Island Sounds: 2006*,
"Corpus Callosum" and "I Look at the Loon" in *Long Island Sounds: 2007*,
"Marks" in *Poet Lore*,
"Rowing at 3 A.M." and "Shoreline" in *The Written Word*,
"I Was Here. This Is Me." "Labor Pool Workers" and "Remember" at *poetryvlog.com*.

A special thank you to George Wallace, who welcomed me, along with countless others, into the poetry community, and continues to mentor and encourage wherever he happens to be in the world. I am grateful to Frank Frankino, who spent years listening to each new poem during lunch breaks; to the members of the LIPC workshop for their passionate love of language; to Charlene Knadle for her wonderful eye for detail; and to Mankh, for his generous, skillful editorial guidance & friendship.

About the Author

Barbara Southard grew up on a canal in Freeport, Long Island. She lived for several years in Woodstock, New York, then Corvallis, Oregon before moving to Huntington, New York, where she and her first husband, Ron, raised their family. Starting out as a painter, she studied under Demetrios Jamieson at Oregon State University, learned intaglio at Ruth Leaf studios, and studied advanced lithography under Dan Weldon at Stony Brook University. Her poetry is a continuum of this lifelong process. She now lives in Miller Place, New York, with her husband, Dan.

Allbook Books *started in 2002 for the publishing of poetry and other writings that encourage one-world consciousness and respect for various cultures, lifestyles and spiritual traditions. The name honors Uncle Alan who was a kind man and a lover of books.*

To receive a catalogue, or for more information regarding books, poetry readings, tutorials, apprenticeship, haiku workshops, the art of Chinese calligraphy, text and graphic layout services, or for further information:

www.allbook-books.com
mankh@allbook-books.com

Allbook Books
PO Box 562
Selden, NY 11784

~ ~ ~ ~ ~